The D

MW00774890

Wick Poetry First Book Series
Maggie Anderson, Editor

The Drowned Girl

Poems by

Eve Alexandra

The Kent State University Press

Kent & London

© 2003 by Eve Alexandra
Library of Congress Catalog Card Number 2003012881
ISBN 0-87338-786-4
Manufactured in the United States of America

07 06 05 04 03   5 4 3 2 1

The Wick Poetry First Book Series is sponsored by the Stan and Tom Wick Poetry
Program and the Department of English at Kent State University.

Library of Congress Cataloging-in-Publication Data
Alexandra, Eve, 1968–
    The drowned girl : poems / by Eve Alexandra.
        p.   cm.—(Wick poetry first book series)
    ISBN 0-87338-786-4 (pbk.: alk paper)
    I. Title.   II. Series.
PS3601.L358D76   2003
811'.6—dc21   2003012881

British Library Cataloging-in-Publication data are available.

for

Sylvia

Done with the Compass—

Done with the Chart!

What's a girl like you doing in a place like this?
That's what I'd like to know, what are we all doing in a place like this?
  —Joy Harjo

There is no feminine outside language.
  —Jacques Lacan

Contents

Acknowledgments

Grateful acknowledgment to the journals in which these poems first appeared: "The Drowned Girl" and "Heroine," *The American Poetry Review;* "Botanica," "The Drowned Girl," "Girl," "Heroine," and "Passage," *American Poet;* "Anatomy" and "The Exchange," *The Pittsburgh Quarterly;* "The Means of Production," *The Harvard Review;* "When I Was Crazy," *Central Park.*

Thank you to my family for their love and support. My deepest gratitude to my parents, Dorothy Martinez and Michael Armstrong. Thank you to Sylvia Parker for everything, every day; and to our beautiful baby Greta and beloved Romeo. I want to acknowledge the many friends whose invaluable insight has furthered my work. Most importantly Marilyn Annucci, whose eye and heart helped shape many incarnations of this manuscript, and Kathleen Veslany for her wisdom, humor, and compassion. I want to thank my teachers at Sarah Lawrence College and the University of Pittsburgh, in particular, Toi Derricotte, Ed Ochester, Catherine Gammon, and Paul Kameen. And above all, I am indebted to Lynn Emanuel for her generous support and her incomparable vision. Thank you to Maggie Anderson for her careful attention and to Alice Cone and the staff at The Kent State University Press for all their hard work. And finally, thank you to C. K. Williams for this honor.

Foreword by C. K. Williams

Erotic disclosure has from poetry's very beginnings been an obsession and a challenge. From Sappho to Donne to the so-called confessional poets of our time, there has always been the finest line between sensual revelation and those much more usual crass recountings, which instead of exalting the complexities of psyche and body, coarsen and demean them. Rare in any age is work that incorporates a passion for experience, a commitment to truth, an ability to plumb the irrational, and a fluency in poetic language and music that can work through all these tangled thickets, but Eve Alexandra does just that.

The poems in *The Drowned Girl* can be frightening in the frankness with which they confront and scrutinize the physical and spiritual ecstasies and terrors the sexual demands of us. While the book deals with other themes, sometimes dire, sometimes less so, it is the poetry of extreme feeling that defines Alexandra's aesthetic, but in all her work she is at once meticulous and effusive, and she has evolved a singular poetic music in both verse and in prose to elaborate her vision of the ardent consciousness.

Informed by so much intensity, the boundaries between *truth* and *fiction* can often seem to be brought into question in her work. Are all the sad and frightening and even occasionally humorous adventures that beset the *I* in this book the experience of the actual person who has written the poems? Sometimes one isn't sure; sometimes one hopes not. Certain poems frankly proclaim that they are speaking of or through someone else's experience, and one is almost relieved to hear it.

But finally none of that matters, because this is true poetry. It immediately takes its place as a participant in the vast historical voice that composes poetry—a voice that contains ten thousand tones but takes nothing into itself that doesn't resonate, as do the poems of *The Drowned Girl*, with authenticity and fervor.

I

The Drowned Girl

This is a quiet grave. It is not made of myths, of great barbarous fish, of coral, or salt. No one submerges himself with metal and rubber, no one shines her white light along the floor. Search parties have been suspended. There is no treasure buried here. This is the place of what-is-not. Of a green so green those flying above it would call it blue. Of a black so black it glows. This is a world with its own species of ghosts—plankton drifting inside her, the barnacles nesting on her hips, her wrists, their whole beings mouths frozen in horror. Sound turned into silence—like cloth on the floor is the shed skin of the lover. Like sheets bereft of the shapes that slept. Once upon a time, she was all escape—her long hair, siren of copper and cinnamon, burning a comet behind her. Her long legs loved heels and short skirts, craved the hard slap of the city beneath her. You would have read this girl. You both wanted more. But she doesn't remember how she got here, in this bed that consumed her. Why she can't put her lipstick on, why one would press color like a promise to the lips. It must have begun with red. But the beginning of this story is lost to the water, you could rake its bottom of leaves and sticks like tea, you could spear one of its last trout and study the slick pages of its intestine. The girl is leagues and leagues away from the first kiss of prologue, but she, throat caked with mud, white skin scaled verdigris, must be the message within the bottle. Words grow in her belly. It doesn't matter who put them there. If they are the children of plankton, descendants of eels and pond scum. They come to her as twins, triplets, and septuplets, whole alphabets swimming inside her. Each one is a bubble, a bread crumb, a rung to climb to the top. And as she ascends she names them with names cradled inside her. Her feet kick and her arms clutch. Her body strong and slippery, a great tongue that propels her: *A is for apple, B is for bone, for boat, C is for candle, for cunt, for cut.*

False Prophets

The first time he comes
I am fourteen,
a good girl,
sitting up straight in algebra.
There is a hole my mother
forgot to finish between my legs.
It's small, but he slips in,
swift with power, curling
into my ear: *Stop,*
put your pencil down.
Do what I say
or your little brother
will die, walking home
from school today.
Are you God? I ask the voice.
He says, *Don't talk back,* so I obey.
He is hungry for small treasures, morsels
of my soul really, but I'm young,
there's some to spare.
He sets up rules—I follow:
each finger must kiss the stove,
double-triple check all locks,
run barefoot through the snow.
He loves me too, he protects me:
Be discreet, people will think you're crazy
if they know. I master my tasks,
so he will leave me alone,
but he comes back. This time
he speaks with a human face,
pockmarked, haloed with pubic hair.
I am full of holes,
and he is the youngest brother
of the town's most famous rapist.
I should smile, be nice.
He sits behind me, junior year

in art class. I remember to smile,
feel sorry for him, be nice.
At night he comes into my head: *Whore,*
take off your nightgown. This is my bed.
I know this game—obey
or he will kill my mother.
My head hurts a lot; it's tight,
so little oxygen left in there.
I fight back when he tells me:
Kill the baby.
I'm baby-sitting; she's asleep
in her crib. He rapes
some little girl too,
has to leave school.
I get an A in art class,
learn sanity is silence.
I will have an operation.
They will open my breasts,
and the doctor will come in.
Dear, he says.
He is here for a full meal.
His words grow huge inside my skull;
I will have to arm myself,
sew these holes with hair
from my own head, set fire
to my intestine, sharpen my teeth.
I will force him out.
I want to grow up now,
to be the voice that speaks
inside of me: *I'm good,*
I'm good.

Notes on Desire

She tries to remember the origin of her desire. This child. This match. This tower. This tango. This sweat. This snare. This noose. This falling. This sleep. This voice in her head. *Scent.* Scent on her. This falling. This sweet. This weight. This crawling on her cunt. This arson. This mouth. This never-enough. She is afraid. To be in the same room with him. She is always. In the room with him. They are making the bed. Her lover's quilt. Heirloom. This room. This house they are building. This *home is where the heart is.* This never-enough. This constant. This voice. This *please go away.* This wife. This bitch. This bad girl. His shoulder. His red shirt. His work hands. His breath on her. They never suspect. In school she learns the names. For what's inside her. *There are five senses: sight, sound, touch, taste, and smell. Scent.* Scent on her. She likes these five senses. In the first year. They made love. Now they fuck. She comes when *she* calls her *bitch, whore, my little slut.* She worries. Gets better and better. She doesn't want to ever go back. To love. To soft. She came into the world like this. A child with the knowledge of her own sexual power. She is wearing pink overalls. She is standing. Her chin resting on the rail. Her hands. Clutching the bars of her crib. Maybe that's why it happened. Maybe he smelled it on her. She was twenty-one. She said *Yes, yes.* It was summer. In trees. By the water. No moon. No stars. Just dark. The dark and their tongues. Their eyes. Their hands. Their scent. It's not always. Like this. Between women. Not always pretty like this. But just this once. It was dark. Hands. Tongues. Breasts. *Scent.* It was the first kiss. *I love you. Scent.* Scent on her. His breath. Work hands. His red shirt. *There are five senses.* She said *Yes, yes.* She is this child. This match. She is this tango. This tower. This snare. She is this falling. This voice. Voice in her head. Falling. Sleep. *Scent.* Sweet. Heirloom. This room. This arson. This crawling on her cunt. She wears red. On the lips of her mouth. Bitch. Bad girl. Never-enough. It was the first kiss.

The Catch

I wanted to ride
in your pickup across the frozen lake,
my body almost seduced
into a tin and scrap-wood shanty,
my warm exhale of wanting suspended
below zero in the space between us,
words frozen, useless.
Language will never reveal
such secrets: how to build a fire
that won't melt the ice; how clumsy,
half-drunk men cut perfect circles
four feet thick. Tricks of the trade
remain physical. I'd have to surrender
to murder myself. I'd have to come inside the shanty,
and it's this simple: because I loved you
I wouldn't. I think of you,
your heart a tackle box
full of jewels and knives for gutting.
And I wanted to open that heart,
to walk on water, but you
are an impossible fate, a man
with a rough tongue and brutal hands,
so much larger than hers—the other swimmer,
the one I've sworn to love.
What do we do when you carve
the circle, bait your hook,
feel the tug and pull, and get
that rare trout, the one who's swallowed
a small fish, and I am she,
that fish with the other inside,
my two selves, the two lovers,
and how will we choose
who will eat this winter
and who will do the killing?

When I Was Crazy

When I was crazy, my mother picked me up
in June for summer vacation, and we drove upstate
to Saratoga, to a mental hospital.

I sat in the back seat and carefully applied my makeup.
When I was crazy it was important to look good.
I wore a new dress to the hospital.
When I was crazy I enjoyed being beautiful.
I was 5'10", 134 and ¾ lbs.
I didn't ask my mother any questions.
I didn't make any demands.

When I was crazy, I heard voices, but I studied very hard.
When I was crazy, I loved any bridge over a highway.
When I was crazy, I was still a good girl, but I was very, very sad.

The hospital was ugly. It's on a road lined with lilacs,
past the racetrack. The hospital was very quiet.
My mother and I crossed our legs
as we sat in the room with a doctor. (When I was sane
I wanted to rip out his guts.)
A nurse brought me warm Pepsi to drink,
in a paper Pepsi cup.
We were having an interview.
I wanted to see the other crazies.
I did not want to dance or make crafts.

When I was crazy everyone said I was crazy. I said, *Please
excuse me, I have to go the restroom* (when you are crazy
it is important to be polite). I went downstairs to pee.
I locked myself in the bathroom, but I did not pee.
I stared into the mirror, and I prayed to myself,
I will not suffer delusions.
I tell my mother, *If you don't get me out of here,
I will never speak to you again.*

I start to talk about things she would like to forget.
My mother is crazy, but she is a good mother;
she doesn't hand me over to the doctor.
Ladylike, we smile and thank him for his time. He is sad
we are leaving so soon. *Come back anytime,* he says.
I never saw the other crazies in Saratoga.

When I was crazy, we left the hospital and went out for lunch.
I had chilled berry soup and a croissant, dripping with honey.
When I was crazy, it was good.
On the way home, I loved my mother and the perfect hope
of cornflowers, born over bridge
over highway. *When I was crazy*

it was good.

The Means of Production

I won't tell you how I came to that table. I won't tell you it was simple: the brownstone, his suit, the flowers, the tea. No address, city, or street. One kiss. I won't tell you he asked. My real name. I never said *Yes. Eve.* I won't tell you about the man from Spain. I won't tell you I loved. You ask *how could she?* All I can tell you is *it was easy.* How I came to that table. He paid for my cab—he said *a pretty girl like you shouldn't.* I won't tell you I was safe. I said. I did it willingly. This man I loved. Carlo. There was the money. I won't tell you the money I made. I can tell you it went smoothly. It was a business transaction. There are rules. I won't tell you. You want always to know. Details. Specifics. They do not exist in that brownstone. That table. Roses. A crystal vase. Good crystal. *A smart girl like you.* I will tell you it was business. *You know.* The money was good. I want you to understand it was easy. A business transaction. I won't tell you it was his idea. There is no *why. A good girl.* His hands. Money. It was easy. This man I loved. I was safe. Clean. One time he said it. I won't tell you he had contempt. I won't tell you it didn't turn him on. Carlo. There is no *why.* I had a kind of control. His hands. One moment. One button. Undone. I wore an ivory blouse. *Yes, Eve.* I won't tell you. Carlo. The brownstone. The cello next door. I won't tell you this is fiction. How much it cost. Silk. His hands. It was very clean. What I want you to understand. One kiss. I won't tell you I loved. The man from Spain. His hands. I won't tell you this is fiction. Undone. I had a kind of control. It was expensive. I want you to understand. He served me tea. Yellow roses. His tongue in my mouth. I won't tell you *it was an accident.* My real name is *Eve.* One kiss. I can't say. *This is fiction.* Undone. One kiss. *It was easy.* A crystal vase. Good crystal. A skirt on the floor. I won't tell you the money I made. I won't tell you *I loved.* He had contempt. He said it once. My legs. The roses. The cello next door. There are rules. I loved. One moment. One button. Undone. I can't tell you *this is fiction.* My skirt on the floor. His hands. Parting my legs. My mouth. It was a business transaction. Expensive. Silk. Don't say you're not turned on. *Tell me.* One kiss. You have contempt. Say it. *A pretty girl, a smart girl like you. Like you.*

H. R. H.

She has popped out of the pages
of the pop-up book. Not unlike the voluptuous
blossom of corn, but more like a horse,
a dappled gray horse
through the gates of its paddock
in the wake of an August storm,
like the scent of tobacco
left by a lover
you never kissed.

Only this piece of her, this blue silk exists,
torn by your thumbnail turning
the pages toward the sweet breath
of her skirts, wanting the extraterrestrial
underneath, the sweet blonde
of a blonde spun into gold
by the fingers of a thousand Rumpelstiltskins.

Night is a tunnel in Paris, France,
the gold's gone black.
Black, black, black, the spoon's silver echo
in the heart's empty bowl.
Your hands are chafed and cold,
my little callus. Where are your mittens?
Where is the happy end? Girls
dream they are called to the dance floor,
worthy and scrawny
handkerchiefs,
just enough lace for her hem.

Sleeping at The Plaza

There were tiny hounds sniffing out their gilded cages. Fireplaces chaste, unlit and beds soft as the pears I ate from palms outstretched. The hem of my dress was wet from the fountain, and finally it lay on the floor like the slick blue skin of a fish. We danced silver as a shiny hook. I heard them clap: red nails flashing smiles. One misplaced kiss, one eye shut. The concierge, bald and fat, cuddling his little pink prick. The elevator stuck. The city was singing. Someone was taking pictures. My legs splintered at the hips, and that night New York wrecked and swelled inside me. A beautiful girl is a great storm slapped around by the hands of her own desire. She lifts up the green skirt of Central Park, wading twelve floors below, and wishes once more for coachman and carriage: to be salt and tear in the horse's eye, to dissolve beneath his blinders.

Exile

Hull white as bone,
no more compass, no more tongue.
The dory rocks like a Ouija,
wings beat. Choirs of anemone
open and close, fish flash their metallic pinks,
their ancient greens. *There at starboard—*
flotsam and jetsam, sirens twitch and shimmy.
Not quite Ophelia, hair tangled
and ghostly as weed, but the wind, the wetness—
it is a kind of death. The old words
stream out in her wake, until she is empty,
shoreless and naked. And she is coming,
silence is coming
the great blue body beneath her salty
and steady as a lover.

II

The Wake

Because there was no other place
to flee to
I came back to the scene of the disordered senses
—Anne Sexton

We all have traces of schizophrenia in us. That's what her shrink had said to her—years ago. Karen, the one with the leather pants and the Akitas. The one who hadn't said much. The one in New York, the one when she was eighteen, then nineteen, and then twenty, twenty-one. Just a girl, really. Although at the time, the girl would insist on *woman.* She was in love with Carlo then, the junkie, the Dutch boy from Spain. Though they never made love. Though they never made it. And she was going to be a movie star. Seriously. She was that beautiful. Martin Scorsese stopped her once. On the street. That was the plan. Don't be deceived. She will get self-righteous and give you all sorts of political reasons for *why.* But in truth she was afraid. She copped out. So this is a story with words and not pictures. Beginning in the rain. On a Friday night in the wasteland of the near-Midwest. With a woman too good for her asleep in the other room. *Just a very associative mind* Karen assures her. *Just.* And she loves her. And that's too pathetic really. Too pathetic to talk about so she'll stop. *Love* like *Mommy.* Not love like Carlo. And never like her, the woman too good for her, asleep in the room. But now that she's said it, at least let her distinguish between the two. Mother as opposed to lover. Try to avoid the clichés of mental illness. It's a rule. She'd said *We can give you a diagnosis if it'll make you feel better.* God, she was too supportive. *We*— like we'll do it together. How would we choose? Hysteria, Obsessive, Compulsive . . . so many beautiful names for girl babies. Still she couldn't trust her. She wasn't an eyewitness. She didn't truly understand. *Seeing is believing.* She'd never seen her like this. When it hit. And later she could barely say *she'd seen she* like this. She would try to remember. To say it backwards. Believe. Have faith. But it was good to sleep. And her lover. Who had been there to witness would say *hush.* The only other ever to see it (except her mother, and that was a very long time ago). Grace loved her and would put her to bed. Kiss her and call her *baby.* And rub her head. Her own sweet head. *My angel. My good girl.*

Promise.

Promise. To tell no one. Grandmother said. Some stuff is even above family gossip. Even when gossip holds us all together. Because we don't call—except on holidays and birthdays—and we don't write letters. Even you who are supposed to be a writer *(And for God's sake, don't write about this).* So sad about Elizabeth. And this time it's not just another baby. My grandmother reminds me: *three babies, each with a different father.* She reminds herself. Crosses herself against the ghost of her eldest daughter's husband. Long after he disappeared, his blood haunting Elizabeth and her brother. Their genes exuding a faint odor. Of the factory. Of work done with hands. Best to blame it on an outsider. Below her. The stench. That's what my Aunt Linda and my grandmother had found. At Elizabeth's. Consuming the house she rented on the outskirts of Poughkeepsie. Like good women of Irish stock they did not flee to the safety of the Holiday Inn, but had stayed. They would sleep on that couch. To show her that they loved her and they would not give her up. My aunt slipped off the diamonds a more appropriate husband had given her. She tucked them into a pair of socks in her suitcase. She started with the bathroom (in case she should have to go). My grandmother cleaned the girls. She cut off their tangles. The nests of birds. I hear about it like this. A war that was fought. My cousin, her landscape decimated. My Lizzie the invisible, the vanquished, the indigenous. Lizzie one year older. Lizzie smart. Lizzie the good girl. Lizzie who slept with curlers in her hair every Saturday night. So she'd have curls for church. Lizzie praying. Lizzie confirmed. Lizzie beautiful too (maybe more beautiful than her cousin). But she'd never wanted to be anything. Nothing that I can remember. Except that once she'd wanted to be a princess. In India. Some weird story we'd read. Romanticizing *suttee* for little American girls. Better than Cinderella. But fire was never her style. Too much wanting. Lizzie refused such desire. The one she loved best was about being buried alive. The princess wore a beautiful dress. And she never screamed or tried to claw her way out. Lizzie said. *She was at peace.*

Grace had read somewhere that in this state (which was now their home) any person could petition that another person be declared insane (a danger to herself or others) and have that person committed to a mental hospital. It seemed crazy. Her beloved shrink back East said, *She must be confused.* But listen: A friend told Grace about this woman. Two women. This wife. Who was actually going to testify against/in support of the insanity of the student of her husband. A student she had nearly adopted. A motherless girl of twenty-one. The same student she had once drunkenly confronted with fucking her husband. But that was years ago. When the girl was very young. Only eighteen. And the wife and the professor had gone to therapy. And the motherless student had become like a daughter to them. A motherless daughter. The husband would make great feasts. Bouillabaisse over meaty slices of his wife's home-baked bread. Stuffed eggplant. Cardamom cake or flan. They would sit on the back porch and smoke after eating. They would drink the best red wine and laugh in the heat of the flowers. The lovely garden. Clematis and blue hydrangea. Giant poppies. Until one August evening the girl takes a cigarette from her lips, extinguishing its tip on the curve of her breast. Burning through the blue dress (borrowed from the wife) into her own inviting skin. The air acrid with the smell of burnt flesh. Erasing the flowers. The clematis and blue hydrangea. Starburst lilies. The dahlias and giant poppies. The girl smiling, feeling herself, using two fingers and the circular motion of the breast exam. She strips off the dress in front of them, seeming to sigh with pleasure, moving gracefully into the heart of their garden. The motion-sensitive light illuminates her defiant gait, her strong back, her hips, her arms arabesque, smooth calves and muscular thighs. Constellations litter her skin. Planets feast on this girl. The wife quickly counts what seem like cartons. She thinks of her own always disappearing Camels. The girl's painted lips bumming one and then another. The peculiar sex of her inhale. She looks for the first time away from the dancing girl and into the blue eyes of her husband. She wonders if he has made love to these planets. If his tongue has lingered on the raised surface of her wounds. Where the constellations begin. Where they end. She hates him, but still wants this child. A child who plays with matches. Sweet. Sweet Pyromania. She will see to it that the girl is safe. Her duty as a woman. Safe from matches and safe from men. After all. Once upon a time she had majored in clinical psychology. And so the wife petitions the court. To save this woman. This girl who was now like a daughter to her. But the student acquiesced. She saved herself the public humiliation. The crucible. She confessed. To being crazy.

The professor is a famous writer. You have read him. He will write a story and make money off the crazy girl someday. He'll be reading right around the corner. At your favorite bookstore. The good one. Not the megastore. But the one run by the local couple. The failed poet and the bibliophile. The professor is charming. His beard still red and impressive. You are reminded of one of Chekhov's men. Masha's officer. Or is it the good doctor? Which Masha? *Which way to Moscow?* We're too late. *We shall never go.* Shake his hand. A cappuccino for your conscience. There's typing as we speak. She hears the keys biting down *(his teeth too hard on her nipples, his teeth too hard on her clit)* from her room. His words poisoning her. Mixing *true* and *false* inside her. Her mastermind. Her said crazy mind that was once open, like a waterbird, with the wingspan of lilies, born of doors unlocking, tiny dollhouse rooms collapsing into each other. Into each other. Other *mother. Mommy, mama , ma. ma. ma.* The moon on the girl's breast seems to glow in the dark. She dreams. The wife dreams the full moon follows her. It keeps pace with their car, she is small and blonde again, her face pressed to the glass of the backseat window. She turns to ask her mother *why*—wherever they go the moon follows them. Only it's not her mommy, but the girl. The girl is driving. Recklessly. Suddenly she pulls off the road. Unbuttoning her blouse as if to breastfeed. She orders the child/wife to climb over the seat. The wife is wet with hunger, willing her mouth to the girl's nipple. Instead of milk she's fed fire. She screams herself awake, covering her mouth with her hands. That's where it ends. *Again and again.* The wife opens a shelter for runaway girls. Occasionally she'll bring one home for dinner.

I am a thief. This story does not belong to me. I am as bad as the professor. Stealing words like bread from the mouth of the girl. The crazy girl. Whom I know—friend of a friend. I have met her. We have spoken. And I too was in love with the girl. From afar. Far away. A voyeur. Wanting her craziness. Loving her for it. Wanting to crawl inside her mind. To be Alice. In her wonderland, too big for her dollhouse. The tiny rooms collapsing. Into each other. Into me. With all my good intentions, I have broken her chairs. I have spilled her tea. I am a jealous lover. She can't have it. This disease. All to herself. I wanted to say *I understand. Me too. Look at me.* How can I say? I wanted both. To rescue her from it and to take it from her. Some nights I prayed. She would come to me. I would hold her. I would be as good as Grace. Say *hush.* The path of my hands through her hair would ease her mind. I would say two things. To her. Both. *It is okay to be crazy* and *but you are not.* They have told me. She hears voices. And I have answered *Such luck.* I too would put my lips to the moons of this girl, but my lips would cool her breasts.

She did not come. She would not. And how would she know? We don't speak of such things. How would we begin? Form the first sounds? Spill such vowels? It is another tired example. The failure of language. The cruelty. Of words. Maybe that's why we prefer the body. Think of the strength of bones. The color of blood. The force of flesh. The body's relentless drive to communicate. The endless conversations of nerves. The chatter of cells. The bastard tongues of DNA. My fists shout at my head. I've tried to explain it to Grace. I'm trapped, and I want so much to escape. Last week a friend and I walked back to work after lunch. We work in a tower. At the university. People occasionally throw themselves out the windows. It happens mostly in the spring. The tower has over forty floors. So they are always successful. They die. I upset my friend. I say these people (mostly women) are brave. I say *I hope* they love their dance into death. I think of them often and wonder. If it feels fast like a roller coaster. Like fucking in a back alley. Drunk. With someone you shouldn't. Or slow and full of longing. A first kiss. A Petipa ballet. *I would wear a red dress.* With a full skirt. It would balloon up. Swallow me. A monster tulip. A poem. A scream. *The butterfly owns her now. It covers her and her wounds. She is not terrified of begonias or telegrams but surely this nightgown girl, this awesome flyer, has not seen how the moon floats through her and in between.* I would glow in the dark. I would be almost. Happy.

She is upset. She disagrees vehemently when I say *It takes guts.* She says it takes guts. To stay alive. And I can't disagree, but I think these dancers, these awesome flyers deserve some recognition. I have to empa-

21

thize. My friend was a friend of the most recent daredevil. Another woman. A baker who baked great cakes. I did not know this woman. What made her so sad. Why she would be so brave. Why she would slip on the red dress. What fabric it was—simple cotton. Or velvet. Or silk. Chiffon. Did it button down the front? Three pearl buttons? Buttons of bone. Or zip up the back? Did it slip over the shoulders, did it wrap around her waist, or send a slit up her thigh? Suicides are particular. Every time I lust for death, I see a knife from my mother's kitchen. I am five and sent to fetch it. The handle is smooth and oiled. I carry it in my left palm. The blade toward my body. The strokes I make are up and down. Never side to side. But the knife no longer exists. My mother has a new kitchen. And I have my own shiny weapons. My own cluttered drawers. My friend is upset. Her friend told no one. She was so desperate. To put on the red dress. And how would she begin? And where would she be now? If she had said something? What do we do with the word *Help?* You know this story. The clichés of mental illness. She'd be rooming with the crazy girl. They'd be twins in blue and red. What would my friend say if I said *Help?* Walking back to the tower, to work. After lunch. After pad thai and iced coffee. *Help me. Help me, Celeste.*

I think of the crazy girl. The girl in blue. With her many moons glowing. Each planet a tiny death. A *help me, Celeste.* It's trickier when you don't want to die. Not all the time. Anyway. The girl wants to live. To be full of lilies. Blooming. Born of doors unlocking. Death isn't gutless. But it's not so simple. Not always the missing piece. To the puzzle. What does she do when she wants to escape? The tyranny of the living body. Listen—those cells are at it again. Gossiping. Her veins are singing. Belting out gospel and disco. *Amazing Grace.* And her tired mind says *hush. Enough is enough. Put on the dress.* And the body, leviathan. Amazon. Keeps on. And what do you do with the cakes to be baked? With the Black Forest? With the woman too good for you. Asleep in your room? And every morning. Lizzie says to her three girls: *You are my reasons. For living.* And Masha falls in love with Vershinin. And I thought I could write this story. Hysteria. Obsessive. Compulsive.

So many beautiful names for girl babies. And what is your name? And who is she to you? My fists shout at my head. My own hands beat me. I have to say *stop*. To myself (when Grace is not there to stop me). Which voice says *stop*? Which me says *go*? She is the subject. The object of telling. And she is the narrator. Where does the responsibility lie? Lay? Get laid? My cousin is diagnosed. *Crazy*. Because she doesn't do laundry. She goes shopping when her girls need clean clothes. She spends almost all her money on t-shirts. Pink panties and gym socks. I love Lizzie. For this. For her refusal to do laundry. For her love of shopping. And my grandmother tells me. She must be rescued. *Enough is enough. (And for God's sake don't write about this.)* Lizzie beats her head against the wall. Her own sweet head. But she does not beat her children. For this she would not be. Called *crazy*. For hitting. A small child's body. But for hitting her own she would. She is. The one she loves. Mother as opposed to lover. Compares it to this. She is fond of drawing analogies. She asks if she would beat her daughter. She of course says. *Never*. So why does she hit her self? And she doesn't know. The correct answer. She will try to tell the story. To say it backwards. She will substitute others for herself. She will represent. Others. After all. Once upon a time she used to be an actress. Almost a movie star. She can find the voice. Perform accents. Develop character. A ventriloquist. She will be a girl in a blue dress. She will eat cardamom cakes and flan. Paint her lips and bum a cigarette as she. Spins this story. She will inhale the clematis and blue hydrangea. She will bake cakes. And jump out of windows. She will not tell Celeste. She will have. Three sisters. She is *crazy*. She is *not*. To be trusted.

On Tuesday, October 25, 1994, twenty-three-year-old Susan Smith drowned her two young children. She is currently serving a life sentence.

I. Rescue

This is the plan, Susie:

At midnight, the guards,
bewitched by empathy

                  entrust
their prize jewel to me,
your queer stranger

waiting by the bed of a blue pick up,
a woman with auburn hair
that reminds you of *you,*

                        before prison, *before—*

When I open my mouth
to say *Susan,* your name

is thick, red velvet
on my tongue,

although there is the music

                of keys unlocking,
        and the knife at your heart is not

                    that familiar,

but only the first breath
of morning. *Do you love*

old movies, Susan? It's like we're inside one,
cradled in shadow, near slow-motion.

I want to kiss each of these women,

                    but you
want nothing with gratitude,
no requests to be rescued—

just drifting into the truck,
intent on the cooler of snacks: apples,
a sandwich, what I've read are favorites—
Mr. Goodbar and Diet Pepsi.

The highways are desolate, radio
reception sketchy. We speak
only of the weather,

                    I have broken more than one law
to minister to you,
to be your accessory,

                    angel,
Sweet Angel of Death,

                    now my prisoner
in a world where 74 percent
of America wants you dead.

I can't give you anything you wanted.

Fate *is* cruel—no Prince Charming,
but some kind of a sister,

                              heir
not to a castle, but a cottage
with whitewashed floors
and twin wrought iron beds.

A jar of tulips waits on your bureau.

Down the road there's a store
run by a man who won't ask

                              any questions,
but he sells fresh milk.

Susan, it's quiet here.

There's room for you, but

                              no other children,
although when you're healed
we could adopt a kitten

or a yellow bird.

II. Inversion (Susan questions the poet):

Was your mother a good mother?

                         Yes, she was a good mother.
A happy mother?

                                   I think so. How do you mean, *happy?*

Happy to be a mother? Happy being a mother—and that is something
quite different from love.

                              Yes, maybe. I don't know.

Most of the time. When I was a child

                          I perceived her
as happy, but then when I was eighteen—I had just come home,
from school, for the summer—we were standing

                  in the kitchen chopping vegetables,
and she told me her mother
never touched her as a child,
so that it was hard—even when I

                  was a baby,
to hold me. She would watch
the other mothers, so affectionate,

                       physical

with their children. She'd practice,
forcing herself to touch me.
Her arms aching, straining
toward me, her

              target.

Were you aware of her discomfort?

My only memory is of love.
I try to feel her body, frightened
of me. She was so beautiful—
her hair fell to her waist,

                                 in two braids.
I remember her freckles, her shoulders—
she loved halter tops.
She was luminous,

                   young.

How old was she?

          Twenty. You were nineteen
when Michael was born.

Yes, but this isn't about me.

             Sorry.

Did she want you?

             She had me.

That's not the same thing—

She was a devout Catholic.
Anything else would have been

                           murder.
I got her out of her father's house,
but he wouldn't walk her

down the aisle. Like yours,
her dress was

                off-white,
short too.
No veil. I'd beg her

                to open
the hope chest, to model the dress,

but she burned it.

She burned it?

                Yes, on the gas grill,
after she left my father.

      I did understand
from a very young age,
that she was an unhappy wife,

                if not
an unhappy mother.

Maybe they're one and the same. How easy for you
to believe that you weren't the problem!

                It's not easy.

Why? Did she fuck up? Did your luminous Mommy
lose it, like me?

                Accidents happened,
my mother would just spill . . .
My father was ritualistic: punishment

had the quality of performance.
I'd slowly pull down my pants;
he'd unbuckle his belt.
There was a rhythm, a precision—
a logic, cause and effect.
My mother surprised me—

I never knew why what happened
happened. She would kick me
up the stairs, her arms and legs
flailing, as if she was

beating back fire.

When my father would beat me,
I would feel his belt, but when
my mother beat me, I would feel

necessary.

My father preferred instruments,
but my mother's

only weapon
was herself. The one time she left a mark—
her hand embossed upon

the skin of my back—
I was twelve and had accused her of hating me.
She made me swear, never to say

hate again.
"How could I?" she screamed, "When I grew
you inside? When your skin

      is my skin?"
Standing between two mirrors
I could see the print of her hand,

      blessing
my back.

I understand.

   I knew you would.

What did she say about me? About what I did?

"We all had those thoughts."

     She sends her love.

Pandora

She's in the box. Toy box. Boxing ring. Ring around the rosy, pockets full of posies. And mares eat oats and does eat oats and little lambs eat ivy. So she . . . no, no, she will *not*. She will not eat her curds and whey, she will not be a muffet on a tuffet. She will eat all the bread crumbs on her ticket out of here. She clicks her stiletto heels and wishes for words fine as Cuban cigars, her arm poking out the dollhouse window, her fingers lascivious as the wind, and she pulls herself a mouth red as a cardinal down from the sky, a real red bird with his noisy flirt chirping *good luck, good luck,* so she can be heard, so she can be a noisemaker all glitter and streamers, New Years and little blue stars. She will bleed words quiet as her life, stigmata small as the two little mosquito bites on her chest we'll call breasts, blessed with something like an adjective to make her nipples stand up straight, straight and sharp as paring knives. And everyone's ears vulnerable as fruit. Overripe. Yes, that's what she'd like them to be. Those ghosts of the gilded frames. Her will will be the axis on which they turn. No dress-up. No make-believe. She's grown strong as a curse. Fancy as a virus. Polyphonic. Multilingual. She will write her way out of this one. This boy meets girl. This $2 + 2 = 4$. Furniture. Pots. Pan. The dog. Hydrangea. Nasturtiums. Eating it all. Grandma's bridal gown and the Christmas tree just vitamins to her. Catalogue her. Call her anything you want. She can't sit here forever, pretty as pages, your good book on the shelf.

Passage

Tiny jewels of sand and salt spill from her mouth. Her lips lie like cloistered nuns. But her ears—they open like lilies. And suddenly all around her there are songs being sung. New notes slick and green, currency on everyone else's tongue. Her own was slow, cut from the wrong cloth, it hadn't been out on the town in years. When it slipped out it wore shoes of cordovan and danced the old dances like somebody's grandmother. There had been a book like the big screen. She had slept for years on pages of silk and sweet organza. Her legs opening fields of lavender and white space. And the babies. It's true she had wished for them. But this chapter she had wrapped tight, kissed their little heads and left them sleeping. She was prepared to be a murderer, to be the worst kind of woman, if that's what it took. She would alter her best black dress and make it new. She would pray for red shoes. She who had chattered away inside her own mind through miles of salt and sea was not afraid to dine alone. She would go to the finest of restaurants and point to the menu. Her teeth would bite and her tongue would remember: *asparagus, quail egg, tiramisu*. When she cleaned her plate she would stare into it like a mirror, the tiny pond where she had said goodnight to her two sons. It would blink back, her third eye. The city sparkles before her. Oh glory of glass, oh gloss of steel. Waltzing back through the maze of brilliance, past the park and the Public Library, the lions purring, her teeth clicking, the alliteration of old avenues and boulevards, the constellations necking with the skyline, the chambers of her heart glowing now, her blood orchestral, the little cells, the millions clapping—the men she passes, their mouths itching *Aren't you? Do I? Didn't she?*

III

beginning

and beginning and beginning
with love [*sic*]. The green
froth of tulle, the titian tiara
of braids, cocktail
of scratch and sparkle.

and beginning and beginning
somewhere between swing
and sin, stop and go.

go, go, go away
all of you in the aisle seats,
hats and gloves,
mamas and papas, sisters
impressionable as clay. Even you
God. This red is our lonely highway,
our bone to pick, our little rib
growing pink in the hay.

Composition

You are not reading. Text unwritten. The text is inside. This is an outside text. These are the footnotes. These are my feet. Bare and walking toward him. And these are hers. Walking away. These are endnotes. As in night. Late December. Or death. The end, which is also a beginning. Conception. A haunting. A first kiss. A goodbye kiss. An epilogue. Epigraph. Prologue. Log it down. As in keep track. Minutes. Days. Weeks. Months. Daily. Entry. Enter into. Danger. Exit. No—a refusal to exit. To say: *I did it. I chose this. I did it willingly. You've made your bed and now you've got to lie in it.* How do you spell *bed?* What color is it? What did the sheets smell like? Before? And after? I put his hand on my thigh. I understood. Everything. Write everything down. Keep track. As in diary. Secret. As in many. Beginning and never stopping. As in speed. Flight. She is. Walking away. She is swift. She is strong. The human body. Amazing. Motion. This is motion. Words are wheels. Turning. Out of control. This is my mouth. Saying: *Stop. I love you.* This is a place. I have left him. I will never return. These words are hollow. Text is.

One-dimensional. How can I. Explain. She is a place. She is safety. X marks the spot. He is a destination to which I am traveling. These are my feet. Barefoot. Endnotes. Blood in the snow. *Pick up your feet.* Ready. Set. *Go.* The gun goes off. There are no false starts. Run eight laps around the track. Run through the field. Run home. Many miles. We have traveled. Together. Six years. I owe her this much. Pack. Pack it up. Logistics. The logic of boxes. Of boxes marked *kitchen* and *picture frames.* And *Christmas.* Ethos. Ethology. Etiology. Epidemic. Epilogue. Log it down. Logic. Love. Love always. *P.S.* You dwell. Only in my body. The body of this text. Which is nothing. And everything, *my love.* My love for her. And this is me. My feet walking toward. These are my hips. This is the will to be carried. This is the stone. *Strike the match.* This is blue light. The will to destroy. These are my own cells. Dividing. As in divisible. As in division. These are my fists. Against my head. These are her hands. This is how they open. Inside me. This is treason. This. Simple act of pen to paper. The type-

face. The little zoo. Of charac-
ters. The decadence of fonts. Of
erasing. Or saving and making it
so. This is the file marked (   ).
This is the slow dirge of conso-
nants. The betrayal of vowels.
The ineptitude. The clumsiness.
The infertility of language.
While the body is motion. A
butterfly. A backstroke. A game
of Russian Roulette. The barrel
spins something beautiful. It
clicks like his heart. Beats inside
my own chest. Her hands on my
breasts. Inside me. Her fists in-
side me. Never open. Never
striking my face. This is the
safety. Of textual violence. I can
lie. Say: *metaphor*. What if I told
you: *this is fiction*. A make-believe
alphabet: breasts, lips, shoulders,
clit, cock, thighs, wrists. . . .
Merely tools for building. They
are images. Substitutions. I am a
substitute for *she*. There is no he.
No translation. No room for
him. Inside me. Inside us. Two.
The two *she*s. Plural. Past perfect.
On my knees. As in I've dropped
to my knees. I'm unzipping his
pants. I want *him* in my mouth. I
want to speak. Fluently. As in
fluency. His hands on my hips
swimming. Toward the mouth of
my thighs. Swimming is the

body. In perfect motion. As in
perfection. As in predilection.
She was afraid of the water. I
told her *trust*. I dreamt he came
to me. We weren't alone. The
pool was full of children. Taking
lessons. Take me from behind.
Under water. The chlorine burns
my eyes. Cleanses the scent of
him. From my body. From the
water inside. She lets go. She is
no longer afraid of the water.
She has a body made for motion.
She is good at sports. Lifts me
above her. Love. See notes below:
This is a love beyond language.
This is the failure. Of my mouth.
Of pen and paper. I try to tell
her: *too perfect for poems*. How
could I begin. To write of our
bodies. I live inside her. How her
blood swims in me. How plea-
sure becomes love. So I beg her. I
need force. To feel her. Other-
ness. To feel her outside. Inside
me. This is the blank page. The
white space. There is no body.
No text. She is written inside me.
He is *other*. As in catalogued.
Classified. As in maps made. I
can tell you about him. I can
spell his name. Measure the span
of his chest. To tell you of the tip
of his cock. Bruised by the red of
my lips. To tell you this color

mixes with the purple swell. Of his skin. To tell you he tastes of metal and salt. To say: *I love him* or *do not.* Technology makes it easy to erase. Or to save everything. Safe. Safety. She is my *X.* My X marks the spot. *Russian Roulette:* the barrel spins something beautiful. Clicks. He must leave the page. Flee my body. This is division. As in divided. This text. Is the unwritten. The forgotten. The unable to forget. These are my footsteps. Each vowel, each consonant crawling toward him. Desire. As in haunt. My metaphor. My mouth. My poetry. She is my own body swimming. She is also the sea. As in *see* her. As in read. Read between the lines. Of my mouth. Of pen and paper. The first kiss. Kiss me good-bye. This is the file marked ( ). You are not reading. Text unwritten. The text is inside.

Sex, Semiotics, Roadsigns, etc.

Attention: there is a curve in the road. A speed bump. She is changing directions. Or taking off her clothes. Chameleon. Speaking. Slipping. There is slippage. And roads are slippery when wet. And so are tour guides and this girl is very. So wet she is wearing a slicker. Like the one she wore the first day of first grade. Bright yellow. So wet she is fluid. Fluidity and fluency all mixed up. Mix you a drink, darling? She'll call you. Try to trick you with that purr, that catcall she calls a voice. Siren. And not the red ones. Not the rescuing kind. No, no. That is paint on her lips. Cheap paint. Nothing electric. She says *green, go.* When you should stop. She'll point you in all the wrong ways. Spread her legs like a map? You'll get nothing but confusion. End up in Topeka or someplace worse. Following all this time, pull-toy. Thinking you had your hands on the wheel. Thinking you got her down. That she might go down on you. Thinking you ride her like those leather seats you got your ass in now—but she was never that car. Not that model you ordered. No import. No export. No pretty baby kept chaste in your garage. She was always off on the side of the road. Fucking strangers at rest stops. Truck stops. Scratching up her skin against the carpet of cheap motels. Setting flares. Flared up. Flashlight. Torch. Her voice haunting you, pulling you close like a guardrail. This wanting consistent as the yellow lanes you live inside of. She is the hum of the Expressway. Chatter mixing metaphor in your ear. You thinking maybe you bought the French translation by mistake. Maybe she is speaking Portuguese. She is speeding up. And slowing down. You are running out of gas in the western West. You some cowboy with a hard-on. Wanting her under the big sky. She will. She will. She will. She is another. A sequel. Part two, to be continued. She is as big as the next page now.

Homecoming

Your fans go wild as you ride into the stadium
in a float on fire with red tissue roses
and a thousand silver stars. When you left the house
your mother said, *You look like a whore,*
but lipstick has to be thick
if it's going to reach
the back rows of the bleachers, catching boys
and girls in your mouth, sucking
on the hard candy of hope.
Queen, you are *too cool*—even the princesses
of this court want to be perfect
as a blonde in blue, sweet
and cold as ice cream.
And that captain out there—the one
who promised you touchdowns,
pretend to love him. This season
is half over, one last June just around the corner,
and you're saving money from two nights a week
and Saturdays at the drugstore for a plane ticket
to some city where nothing is handed to a girl
just for being pretty, a place
where everyone plays hard to get,
and these small town subjects will be forgotten,
appearing only in dreams, like a language
spoken long ago, so take this opportunity to wave
good-bye although it will be mistaken for hello.

Rape

You do not remember how
you got from your bed
to the bathtub. The water is running

and running. He is French,
studying architecture at N.Y.U.
You try to keep your head

above water. When he kissed you
on the swings it was lovely.
You met him at the dance.

You are nineteen, face down
in the water. You don't remember
saying hello, but remember walking

up the hill. His white linen suit.
Three perfect lines of coke. Azaleas
blooming fuchsia everywhere.

It is almost summer. You like strangers.
You are beautiful; you know this,
and he tells you so. Nineteen,

almost twenty, face down
in the water. His penis
is in your vagina. Try to remember,

is he using a condom? You think no,
no condom. Afraid
you will choke. At first,

it was good. Try to remember
his name. The water still running.
Hear the voices of the women next door.

His penis is in your vagina.
Or is it up your ass?
This is what you don't understand:

how you lose track
of your own body. Try
to rise up from the water.

He is holding your hands
behind your back. He is heavy.
Water running and running.

It is too late for *no*.
The azaleas are blooming
fuchsia everywhere.

Remember his face.
You are under water now.
Too late for *no*.

Something is wrong;
he's still hard—the coke.
So hard he never comes.

Your forehead smacks
into the smooth, white hollow.
Play a game, like when you were little,

count how long
you can hold your breath.
Remember your father

teaching you to swim.
You pray he will come,
get off in your asshole.

44

The water is running and running.
Someone's pounding. Your door.
He slows down. They keep pounding.

You thank God. He pulls out.
Tell him to leave now. He tells you
how beautiful you are.

Think about the mess
on the floor. His white linen
all wet. He kisses you

good-bye; you are sure of this.
Azaleas fuchsia everywhere.
Nineteen, almost twenty.

Look for blood, but don't see.
Only scratch marks on your face,
on your breasts.

Only the burning of your wrists.
Open the window. *Go to sleep.*
Later you laugh with your friends

about fucking and flooding
the floor. Your mouth is full
of kisses, of salt

and flowers. You dream
of fish, whole buildings
under water, anything but

the word.

Anatomy

When I think of my father's body,
I don't think of his hands,
the hungry fists of an Irish boy
famous for a left hook
that brought him a national title
and bloodied our noses, medaled
our skin in furious beatings.
I don't think of the white soles of his feet,
or nights they dropped the dark hulk of his chest
into my bed. I don't think.
I don't see the siren go off at his temple,
the scarlet that could soak him in seconds,
devouring his face. I don't think
of small mistakes—mud on the rug, a tongue that speaks back,
the unfinished plate—veins
raging to the surface of his neck.
I don't think of the lost smallness
of my own angry body, of running
away
and away, my own arms already taut
and expert at blocking, enough
to carry my brother for miles.

When I think of my father's body,
I think of my brother, nineteen and stupid,
the cops with guns at their hips,
the sentence for trafficking a kilo:
three to five. I think of the names of states,
of Maryland and Texas, places they threatened to send him.
I think of my father fighting again,
the gray boxer who stood in that kitchen
the day they told him to relinquish his son.
I think of the warm hull of his back, the spine
and the two arms, the discipline of strength.
I think of the soles of his feet, how they swayed

back and forth, of good-bye built into a cathedral,
his girl and his boy cradled within, his hands
tucking our heads under his chin,
the warmth of his sweat,
the strange surprise of his lips, the softness
slipping out of him, like a song
that slept for years in his bowels,
and I think of the voice of forgiveness,
I think of blood.

Girl

Be careful if you take this flower into your house. The peony has a thousand lips. It is pink and white like the lady's skirt and smells sharp and sweet as cinnamon. There are a thousand ants living inside but you will only see one or two at a time. I am like that down there—pink and busy inside. The dark is a bolt of cloth, crushed and blue, and I unfurl against it. If you lay down on the floor of the closet, the hems of silk will lick you. My own gown is thin as the skin of dried grass so I can see the ants dancing down there. The night has big paws. I imagine the wool of bears, the cloth of monkeys. The night smells like vetiver and cedar. His mouth is cool with mint and warm with rum, and I am not afraid as he rubs his wool against me. I saw the bear dancing at the circus when I was small. He was wearing a green felt cap with gold brick-a-brac and kept by a thin wire thread. My brother bought me a sucker for the train ride home, and I am like that now on the inside burning soft with lemon. *What fruit do you like best?* I like tangerines. And the night leaves me these. A small paper bag on the bedside table. The wrought iron and roses like an altar. I am glowing now. My teeth are stitching kisses to my fist. I go to the river. My legs are frog legs. Tiny wands, see how they glisten. A thousand fish swim through me. I am a boat now. I know no anchor. My hair unfurls, copper and cinnamon. Look how it opens, *beautiful world.*

Unfinished bodies in the dark

My lover slept on the floor
of a one room house
littered with cousins. At night
she practiced making love
with her pillow. Its white down
crushed between her legs,
the slick tip of a cock
growing from the lips
of her six-year old heart.
In the night God makes
no mistakes. This was the way
she wanted it, the boy
with the long black hair
and flat chest touching
his penis. Its small hardness growing
brave enough to hope
for a woman,
hoping against the weight
of what she would become.

The Exchange

I wanted to be on fire with sequins—mercurial,
amphetamine—to have lower Manhattan
reflect off my breasts, to stop cars
with the relentless choreography
of my ass in gold short-shorts,
to make the mouth of the city
curse and swim
for the sheen of my thighs and calves.
I've walked for miles in stiletto heels
without bruising a blister—painted
my lips the red that refuses to bleed
when blowing

kisses. On Friday nights
we would get stuck on the Hutch,
lose ourselves in the entrails
of the Meatpacking district
behind the pirouette of cabs—
johns rushing the concession stand,
manna coming on soft as cotton candy,
sex sticky as rainbow jujubes.
We were the college girls with our faces powdered
and pressed to the tinted glass—the rich ones
in a uniform of black tights and minis.
When men asked my major,
I said *theater.*

Scoring music
and dealers, we would line
the leather of bars, Persephone perched
on stools at clubs where she got in the door
for looking bored and pretty. I spent
five hours in a dressing room
with a band from Trinidad
stoned on something called *blue,*

remember the smoke
rising off all eight of their faces,
rhythm locking into my hips,
but none of their hands. I never
made money off of any it. Mostly
our sex was cool and flat
as those pale green mints
at all-night diners.
Mints tasting like chalk, scooped with the lip
of a tiny silver spoon. How can I tell you

I just want it to be real:
our two bodies breathing,
the texture of cotton,
the toilet,
the brick of the wall.
Now I'm not acting, not selling anything,
and I want you to own me
one blue night like this.

Botanica

They are everywhere—those sunflowers with the coal heart center.
  They riot
without speaking, huge, wet mouths caught at half-gasp, half-kiss.
Flowers she promises I'll grow into, sweet gardener,
long, luminous braids I'd climb like ladders, freckles scattered
across our shoulders in a spell of pollen. She's sleeping there—
  on that table
with its veneer slick as a glass coffin. She's fed us fiddleheads,
  the tiny fists
of Brussels sprouts, cupcakes, even the broken song of the deer's
  neck. Singing.
Flowers everywhere. In my bedroom chaste daisies and the vigilance
of chrysanthemums. Dirt under my nails, pressing my cheek to the
  shag rug
with its million fingers. You could lose anything: a tooth, Barbie's
  shoe,
this prayer. *She loves me. She loves me not.* I stare at my reflection,
  a posy
of wishes. Morning glory, nightshade, tulip, rhododendron.
In this poem I would be the Wicked Witch and she Snow White.
  Waiting.
My father talks to me about their lovemaking. My mouth empty
as a lily. I try to remember the diagram. *Which is the pistil?*
Which is the stamen? Roads of desire circle our house: *Lost Nation,*
  Severance,
Poor Farm. Branches catch the wings of my nightgown.
There is a crow and the smell of blackberries.

Blue

The house is blue, milky and narcotic. The round shingles like petals, a million of them, like a field of glossy oysters with their prize bellies, like chaste lace on the girl's cuff. The trim mother called *gingerbread* haunting the windows, as if carpenters were elves, and the thin scroll of oak could melt in your mouth, spice burning the tongue. The air is thick with hyacinth and lilac, spathes of barbiturate and kiss. The long necks of delphinium with their bells like tiny mouths, tiny veins of forget-me-nots crawling across the slated path, the single scrape of geranium. The back door cracks open like a robin's egg, glossy skin of membrane still clinging. A wool slipper drowns in a pool of yolk. The tiny nest is empty—the bird died, its feathers still wet and leafy lanugo. It slept in the porcelain bowl warmed in the oven. There is no song, just a calico dress and the beat of the girl's heart as she eats her porridge. Her spoon is open like a cyclops looking. It is searching the bottom like a hand reading the floor of the pond. She stays down there a long time. She works hard. She works until her face glows like a halo, cyanotic. Her eyes pearl and gleam. She is not a mechanic, she is a machine. She is the switch flicked on, the *g o*. Oh yes, she can swim now. In the blue water, she is a swan. And there is a promise. A promise circling like a wing inside her.

Heroine

Needle to thread. Scythe to wheat. Foot to pedal. Hammer and sickle. *Work, work, work.* She has three sisters. At dusk she drinks tea. From the silver belly of a samovar. In the dark she drinks vodka. She takes a lover who smells of fresh meat and the pines. The hunt is on him, like his tongue on the crest of her sex. Like the little forest of white down on her breasts. On the nape of her neck. A hunger grows. Grows inside her. *Note: She is not hungry for him. He is a symptom of that hunger. An empty cup she could keep replenishing. A clue: bread crust, apple core, chicken bone.* Wish-bone. *Knowing three languages is a useless luxury in this town. A sort of unwanted appendage. A sixth finger.* She can't remember the Italian for *window.* She climbs the ceilings. The water spouts. She eats strawberries, using her lips like a blind girl uses her fingers. Little match girl. Little lamb. Little shoe. Black boot. *Achoo.* A little red wine? Red Riding Hood. All the better to see you with. To read you with, my dear. *Follow.* Over the river. Through the woods To the sea. Knees deep in the salty water. To the island of Crete. To Tunis. To Florence. To Russia. To Moscow. Finally. *Finally,* you say, to Moscow. She will arrive on that page. That splendid stage of trajectory. Of destiny. Destination. She is splendid. Sexy. *Oh baby.* She is Little Miss Adjective. She will wear her best black dress. Sings a soft song when she walks. Syllables of silk, of organza and tulle say *Hush, we are almost at "The End."* She wears a veil of Swiss lace. *Real,* they said about the lace she was wearing. Little accents, little umlauts, tiny apostrophes like snowflakes sting her cheeks. She does not blush. She makes the sign of the cross. She makes a date. With hunger. With the great black cloak of a train. But this time she doesn't lie down. She refuses to make her bed. To spill her blood like children. She doesn't set herself on fire. She won't sign her name or spell you her secrets. She won't uncross her legs. She opens her mouth instead. She opens her mouth and she. She eats. She eats it all: *porters, nannies with babies, the tracks, the coal, the iron, the ore.* She dines for pages, for chapters. Eating paper, drinking the sweet black ink, wiping her mouth on her sleeve. Then she eats her best black dress and so she is naked. And so she is huge. And it is you, it is you she is holding like an open book, well loved, in her hands.

Note

"The Wake" contains lines from Anne Sexton's "Flee on Your Donkey" and "Song for a Red Nightgown."